MY BODY IS A RAINBOW
The Color of My Feelings

MALLIKA CHOPRA

author of *Just Breathe*, *Just Feel*, and *Just Be You*

ILLUSTRATED BY IZZY BURTON

RP | KIDS
PHILADELPHIA

Running Press Kids
Hachette Book Group
1290 Avenue of the Americas, New York, NY 10104
www.runningpress.com/rpkids
@RP_Kids

Printed in China

Text adapted from *Just Feel: How to Be Stronger, Happier, Healthier, and More* by Mallika Chopra, originally published in October 2019 by Running Press Kids.

First Edition: July 2021

Published by Running Press Kids, an imprint of Perseus Books, LLC, a subsidiary of Hachette Book Group, Inc. The Running Press Kids name and logo is a trademark of the Hachette Book Group.

The Hachette Speakers Bureau provides a wide range of authors for speaking events. To find out more, go to www.hachettespeakersbureau.com or call (866) 376-6591.

The publisher is not responsible for websites (or their content) that are not owned by the publisher.

Print book cover and interior design by Frances J. Soo Ping Chow.

Library of Congress Control Number: 2020939730

ISBNs: 978-0-7624-9904-5 (hardcover), 978-0-7624-9903-8 (ebook),
978-0-7624-9905-2 (ebook), 978-0-7624-9906-9 (ebook)

APS

10   9   8   7   6   5   4   3   2

TAHIRA AND KAVYA

Keep singing, dancing,
twirling, and laughing.
And reminding us to imagine and dream.

Play and seek joy
everyday.

Did you know that your body is absolutely amazing?

Your body helps you explore the outside world and also helps you to know your inside world.

Your body can do many things at the same time. You can move and talk, dance and sing. While your heart beats and your mind thinks, you use different parts of your body to see, hear, taste, smell, and touch.

Your body also helps you feel the feelings deep down inside of you. Have you ever felt butterflies in your stomach when you are scared, heart ache when you are sad, or tingling in your hands when you are excited?

When you know how your body reacts to your feelings, you can control your reactions and feel powerful.

You can use colors, words,
and your breath to explore your body.

Imagine a rainbow. A rainbow has many different colors:
red, orange, yellow, **green**, **light blue**,
dark blue, and **purple**.

You can use your imagination to bring the energy
of these colors into your body.

Sit in a chair or on the floor.
Take a deep breath, in and out.

In and out.

Feel your bottom resting under you.
Do you feel how the chair or floor is strong and stable?
The ground beneath you is always there to keep you safe.

Take a deep breath and imagine the color **red**
swirling around your bottom.

Say, "I am safe."

Choose one hand and place it right under your belly button.
Are there times when you are aware of this area?
Perhaps when you are really excited by something?
Feel how your hand can warm this area with its energy.

Take a deep breath and imagine the color **orange**.

Say, "I am creative."

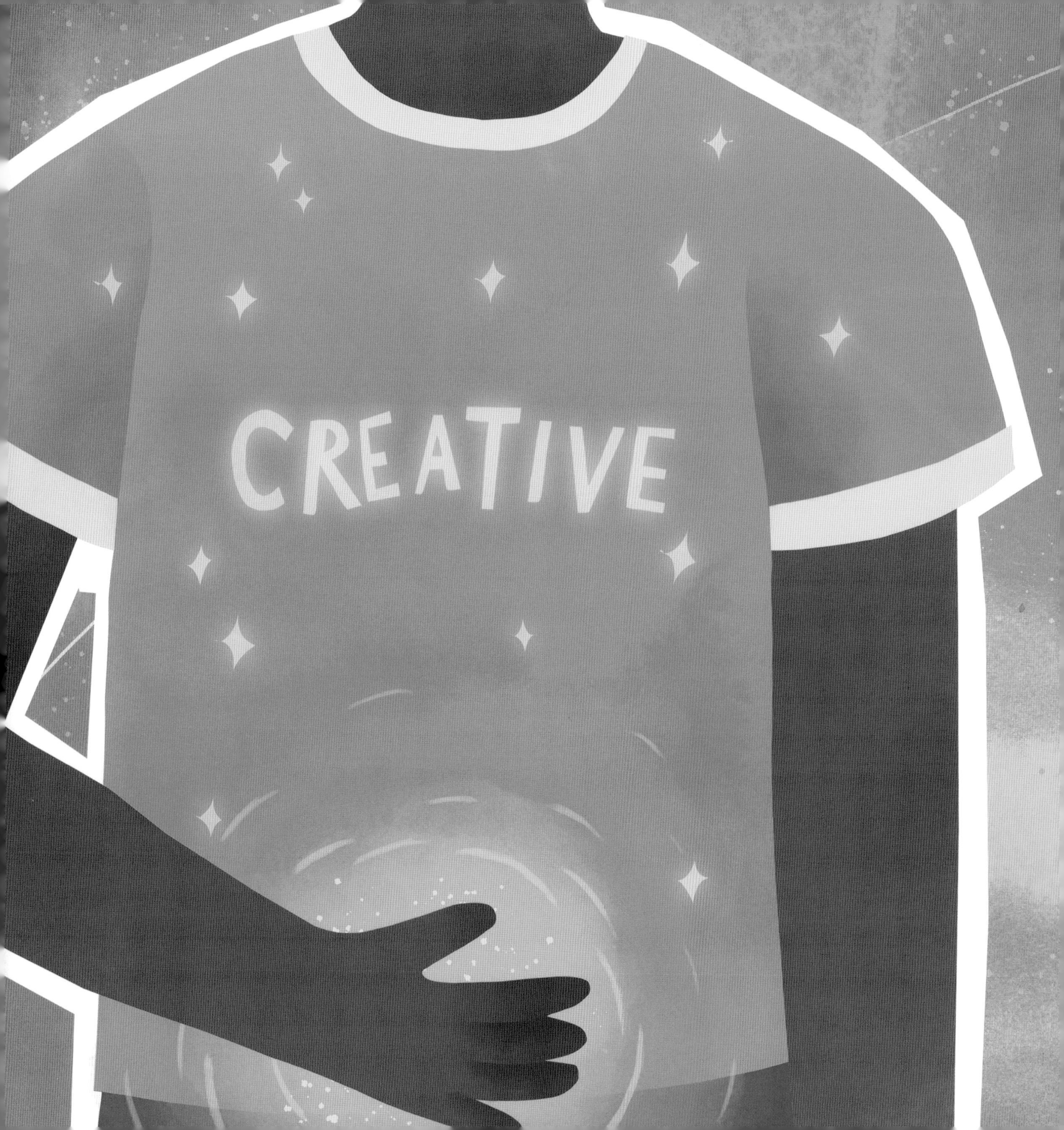
CREATIVE

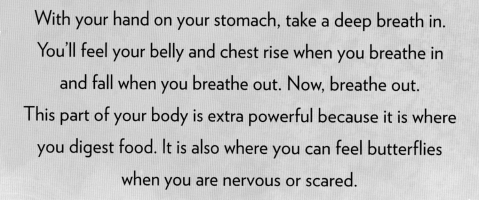

With your hand on your stomach, take a deep breath in.
You'll feel your belly and chest rise when you breathe in
and fall when you breathe out. Now, breathe out.
This part of your body is extra powerful because it is where
you digest food. It is also where you can feel butterflies
when you are nervous or scared.

Breathe in the color **yellow**.
Breathe out.

Feel how the color can warm you
inside in a comforting way.

Say, "I am strong."

Your heart is where you feel love and connection.
You can feel happiness or sadness in your heart.
Place one hand over your heart.

See if you can feel your heart beating.
Imagine the color **green** surrounding your heart,
holding it with kindness.

Breathe in and out.

Say, "I am loved."

Put your attention on your neck and throat.
Your voice helps you tell others what you need
and want to feel happy and healthy.

Do you ever find it hard to tell someone how you feel?
Maybe you try to talk but your throat is dry and feels tight?

Imagine a **light blue** color on your neck and throat,
making you feel cool and calm.

Breathe in and out.

Say, "I am unique."

Place a finger in the space between your eyebrows.
Feel the energy from your finger giving power
to your face and inside your head.

Imagine a **dark blue** color spreading across your face and
inside your head, bringing you a calm power and strength.

Breathe in and out.

Say, "I am wise."

Place your hand on top of your head.
Sit tall, with your back and neck straight.
Feel the strength and pride of your body.

Remove your hand from your head
and see the color **purple** rise above you.

Say, "I am."

Feel the space over your head,
up past the ceiling and into the sky above.

Let the color **purple**, followed by all the colors,
float up all the way to the sky—past the clouds and to the stars.

Breathe in and out slowly.

Think about other parts of your body and imagine
what colors come from them.

Maybe you see **pink** swirling around your fingers
or **brown** around your toes.

You can come up with any colors for your body, and
you can create any phrases that make you feel strong.
Perhaps you choose to say words like,
"I am magic," or "I am happy."

Breathe in and out, slowly.
Imagine your body as a big rainbow, shining and glowing
and full of energy but also peaceful and at rest.

Remember, your body is amazing and is there to help you.
The next time you feel upset, scared, frustrated, or angry
—connect to your body.

Choose a color and feel it in your body.

Say the words to remind you that you are safe, creative,
strong, loved, unique, wise, and perfect just the way you are.